SEVEN REASONS YOUR CHURCH WILL NEVER HAVE REVIVAL

ALSO FROM REVIVAL TODAY

Financial Overflow

Dominion Over Sickness and Disease

Boldly I Come

Twenty Secrets for an Unbreakable Marriage

How to Dominate in a Wicked Nation

Seven Wrong Relationships

Everything a Man Should Be

Understanding the World in Light of Bible Prophecy

Are You Going Through a Crisis?

The 20 Laws that Govern the Financial Anointing

35 Questions for Those Who Hate the Prosperity Gospel

The Art of Spiritual Warfare

Help for Your Darkest Time

Seven Reasons Your Church Will Never Have Revival

Books are available in EBOOK and PAPERBACK through your favorite online book retailer or by request from your local bookstore.

SEVEN REASONS YOUR CHURCH WILL NEVER HAVE REVIVAL

A MESSAGE FOR PASTORS

JONATHAN SHUTTLESWORTH

Without limiting the rights under copyright(s) reserved below, no part of this publication may be reproduced, stored in, or introduced into a retrieval system or transmitted in any form or by any means (electronic, mechanical, photocopying, recording, or otherwise) without the prior permission of the publisher and the copyright owner.

The content of this book is provided "AS IS." The publisher and the author make no guarantees or warranties as to the accuracy, adequacy, or completeness of or results to be obtained from using the content of this book, including any information that can be accessed through hyperlinks or otherwise, and expressly disclaim any warranty expressed or implied, including but not limited to implied warranties of merchantability or fitness for a particular purpose. This limitation of liability shall apply to any claim or cause whatsoever, whether such claim or cause arises in contract, tort, or otherwise. In short, you, the reader, are responsible for your choices and the results they bring.

The scanning, uploading, and distributing of this book via the internet or any other means without the permission of the publisher and copyright owner is illegal and punishable by law. Please purchase only authorized copies, and do not participate in or encourage piracy of copyrighted materials. Your support of the author's rights is appreciated.

Unless otherwise noted, all scriptures are from the NEW KING JAMES VERSION®. Copyright© 1982 by Thomas Nelson, Inc. Used by permission. All rights reserved.

Copyright © 2024 by Revival Today. All rights reserved.

Released: October 2024
ISBN: 978-1-64457-766-0

Rise UP Publications
United States of America

www.riseUPpublications.com
Phone: 866-846-5123

CONTENTS

Introduction	7
You'll Never Have Revival Because… *You Won't Have One*	11
You'll Never Have Revival Because… *You Don't Know What Revival Is*	15
You'll Never Have Revival Because… *You're Not Open to Having Revival*	21
You'll Never Have Revival Because… *Your Staff Hates Being in Church*	23
You'll Never Have Revival Because… *You're a Money Control Freak*	29
You'll Never Have Revival Because… *You Hate the Holy Ghost*	37
You'll Never Have Revival Because… *You Choose Guest Speakers Instead of Evangelists*	39
Afterword	43
Author Photo	46
About the Author	48

INTRODUCTION

This book may not have the most uplifting title, but it contains an extremely important message. Too many people are missing the move of God, and believe it or not, the Devil is not responsible. I've identified seven reasons people and churches miss out on what God is doing on the Earth. These causes address church structures steeped in ritual and religion. I hope this book will help people not only experience revival but be a part of this final move of God.

In His ministry, Jesus didn't spend time rebuking prostitutes, drug dealers, and gang members. He rebuked the Pharisees and Sadducees, who created a structure that forbade the moving of the Holy Spirit. That same system has undergone a remodel but still operates in many churches today. My aim in writing this isn't merely to criticize—although criticism is necessary.

INTRODUCTION

I want to share the perspective of a seasoned evangelist with forty years of successful experience in ministry. He once told me, "In ministry, you don't primarily battle devils—90 percent of your battles are with pastors." I enjoy being able to speak as both an evangelist and a pastor. I'm not a frustrated evangelist struggling to book meetings. I'm also not a disgruntled pastor fighting to get my church to grow.

The growth of Revival Today Church is not a stroke of luck, nor is it solely due to my pastoral skills. My experiences as an evangelist have allowed me to observe and identify barriers to the move of God. As a pastor, I've made a conscious decision to keep those obstructions out of my church. There are no blockades impeding the flow of God's Spirit at Revival Today Church. The truth is you don't have to beg for revival. All you need to do is identify and remove the obstacles that are hindering the flow of God's Spirit. Once these are cleared, the Spirit of God will show up and have His Will.

I travel and preach, and almost every night, people comment, "You must be tired." But I'm not tired. I'm less tired with each passing day because revival is refreshing. But if you battle the things I'm about to share, those battles will drive you out of the ministry.

While the concepts presented in this book are important for everyone to understand, I want pastors and evangelists

INTRODUCTION

to pay special attention to these seven common hindrances to revival. Regardless of your role in ministry, I encourage you to search your heart to determine whether you're perpetuating any of these barriers to revival.

YOU'LL NEVER HAVE REVIVAL BECAUSE...

YOU WON'T HAVE ONE

You simply aren't interested in having a revival. You've fallen in love with your weekly systems, and you cringe at the thought of violating them to usher in revival. Have you ever thought, 'I've been feeling to have a revival, but we can't fit it into our schedule this year.' Royal Rangers, staff vacations, and the like are not good reasons to put off revival.

Pastor Rodney Howard-Browne held a large revival meeting in South Africa in 2023. He ignored the local pastors' warning when they told him no one in South Africa would attend weekday morning services. He proceeded with them anyway and drew a crowd of 2,500 people. How do you tell a guy who's been doing something successfully for thirty years that no one will come? You can know everything there is to know about human behavior and still not be successful in ministry because God doesn't care about psychology or sociology.

Break your routine. Clear a week in your church calendar and have revival. Your small group meetings don't matter more than having a revival. Clear a week off your schedule. Allow your staff to come in late so they're energized for a week of services. Try it. It's not something you're going to do forever. It's a week or two, maybe three or four.

It's good to have systems and programs as a pastor. I have them. We have Wednesday night services and a spiritual emphasis weekend service the first weekend of every month. You should have these things, but you should also pause your regular schedule to bring in somebody who's gifted by God to explode the growth of your church. God will use that person if you give them the freedom to minister. Let them do their thing—don't muzzle the ox while he is treading the grain. God will use that person to bring you twenty years of financial and congregational growth in just a few weeks.

Quit praying for revival and instead invite someone to your church who has revivals. John G. Lake said, "Prayer is often used as a refuge by men to dodge the action of faith." You don't pray for a financial harvest; you sow seed, and you reap a harvest. Likewise, you don't pray for God to send revival, you invite someone full of the fire of God, remove all limitations, and revival will follow. Schedule Rodney Howard-Browne for one week and you'll experience a revival—no prayer required. He carries revival.

When we filled the Pittsburgh Riverhounds Stadium, we didn't do it by praying, "Lord, we believe one day you'll fill the stadium in this city." Don't pray useless prayers like that. Instead, lease a stadium, do the work necessary to fill it with sinners, and have a crusade. Don't wait for God to do things. Take the power that God has given you and get to work. You should be interested in revival.

My dad had a revival in Otisville, Michigan. On Sunday morning, 180 people came. By the end of the sixth week, there were over 800 in attendance. Revival grew the church. After my dad left, the church went from an average of 180 to about 500 members. That constitutes many years of average church growth in just six weeks.

Revival is an acceleration. One of the first revivals I had occurred in Fitchburg, Massachusetts, with Pastor Brian Tomes. There were 120 people present at the first Sunday morning service. As the meeting continued to grow, we continued to extend the meeting. After five straight weeks of revival, we saw over 300 people saved. The church grew exponentially and, as a result, required multiple services. Not soon after, they had to build an addition to the church to accommodate the rapid growth. What was once one of the smallest churches in that Assemblies of God district became the largest church in the district in just five weeks of revival!

YOU'LL NEVER HAVE REVIVAL BECAUSE...

YOU DON'T KNOW WHAT REVIVAL IS

Beware of adages about revival that aren't based on the Word of God. *'Revival is a sovereign move of God.'* No, it's not. God doesn't move sovereignly. The Holy Ghost moves in response to the hunger and desperation of people. He doesn't pick cities at random to pour out revival. I've seen and heard many ridiculous and unbiblical definitions of revival. Before I define what revival is, let me list all the things that revival is not.

- Revival isn't a cloud coming into the sanctuary.
- Revival isn't feathers being shed by angels as their wings decay.
- Revival isn't gems appearing in the carpeting of the church.

Revival is men and women being drawn to God in mass, both in the church and outside the church.

- Revival is people returning to God.
- Revival is people being saved.
- Revival is people being healed.
- Revival is people being baptized in the Holy Spirit.
- Revival is people speaking in tongues.
- Revival is Book of Acts manifestations.

There can be signs and wonders beyond those cardinal doctrines mentioned above, but revival doesn't depend on them. Some ministers can sit and watch 200 people come to an altar and then say, "One day, I believe the glory will come to this church." They have no idea what revival looks like. Healing and salvation are manifestations of the glory of God. If you're looking for a cloud or some spooky experience to confirm that you're in revival, you'll miss the move of God that's happening around you.

Beliefs surrounding revival have two extremes. Some make it spooky and mystifying and in no way practical. Nothing of consequence comes out of it. I've realized there is a large portion of the Body of Christ who would be more excited to see the glory cloud come into the sanctuary than to see a broken family with addicted and bound teenagers set free and filled with the Holy Ghost.

Then there's the camp that believes revival is about souls being saved and *only* souls being saved. Souls coming into the Kingdom of God is a hallmark of revival, but that's not the only aspect of revival. According to the Book of Acts, revival includes devils being visibly cast out and people set free from addiction. Revival is God's presence invading the atmosphere in response to people's desperation, hunger, and thirst. Revival is when backslidden, lukewarm Christians, the type who start putting their coats on as the altar call is given, are set on fire for God again. Revival causes indifference to be driven out of church people. That's why it's called *re*vival. You can't revive something that wasn't once alive.

The Brownsville and Lakeland, Florida revivals with Pastor Rodney Howard-Browne hosted 4,000 people on weekdays and 8,000 at night. After Pastor Rodney dismissed 8,000 people from the weeknight meetings in Lakeland, all the nearby IHOPs and Waffle Houses were filled with church people.

Revival is not a predictable event, but a divine outpouring that can happen anywhere at any time. My cousin, who attended the meetings, had to drive forty minutes from the church to find an IHOP that could seat them at 11 p.m. When he walked into the IHOP, the servers were all out under the power, laying on the floor, speaking in tongues because the glory of God had spread forty minutes away. Many reported seeing the same thing at other restaurants. Some servers were drunk in the Holy Spirit and started crying while they were taking people's orders. Now that is the unexpected, transformative power of revival!

> This became known both to all Jews and
> Greeks dwelling in Ephesus; and fear fell

on them all, and the name of the Lord
Jesus was magnified. And many who had
believed came confessing and telling their
deeds. Also, many of those who had practiced magic brought their books together
and burned them in the sight of all. And
they counted up the value of them, and it
totaled fifty thousand pieces of silver. So
the word of the Lord grew mightily and
prevailed.

— ACTS 19:17-20

The entire book of Acts is a textbook on Revival, Acts chapter 19 especially. It is not a personal experience. In Acts 19:20, Paul shook Ephesus. He preached and taught multitudes and performed unusual miracles. *"So mightily grew the word of God and prevailed multitudes."* The word *multitudes* is used throughout the Bible. God likes big crowds. Heaven has a big crowd. Jesus spoke to big crowds. Peter addressed big crowds.

It's interesting how everything except church is supposed to be big in our society. Home Depot, Walmart, casinos, and baseball stadiums are all expected to be large. The spirit of religion causes people to believe there's something great about being small.

It doesn't make mathematical sense, but one church of a thousand would have a greater impact than ten churches with 200 members each. Ten small churches will easily go unnoticed. But a single group of a thousand Christians is a sign to politicians, local officials, and the entire community that God is present. It's a giant middle finger to the Devil to have a massive crowd of people come together to worship God despite trillions of dollars spent toward university and media programming aimed at stifling the gathering together of the saints.

YOU'LL NEVER HAVE REVIVAL BECAUSE...

YOU'RE NOT OPEN TO HAVING REVIVAL

You are not open to having a revival at your church. You're so attached to your church's systems that you've disqualified yourself from a move of God. You can't have an eighty-minute revival—there's no such thing.

Don't ask an evangelist to preach, give a strong call for souls, lay hands on the sick, baptize the youth in the Holy Ghost, and be finished by 8:30. Revival is a lengthy process. There's praise, worship, preaching, time spent at the altar, laying on of hands, and whatever else the Holy Spirit wants to do on any given night. Don't place your Sunday morning service expectations on an evangelist you invited to spark a revival. Such a ridiculous request makes you appear to have a mental problem. It leads me to believe you have the same concept of time as a four-year-old child. Deep down, you know it's impossible. You're simply not open to revival.

I've heard all the excuses. "Our buses leave at 8:30." Why? Who scheduled the buses to leave at 8:30? Are they rogue buses that leave on their own schedule? Do they operate by AI? No, you scheduled them to leave at 8:30 PM to cap how late the service can go because you want to go home. Tell the buses to leave at 9:30 PM. I'd pay for the extra hour. I wish people would just say what they mean. Just say you're tired. I would much rather a pastor tell me, "Hey, listen, I'm tired, and I don't really like being in church because I've been coming to church for a long time. I've been a pastor for thirty-five years. I'm bored, and I feel like our church has grown as much as it's ever going to grow. I don't care to be in the services. Finish by 8:30 because I want to go home. I have Yellowstone recorded on my DVR, and my wife and I want to watch it together." I'd rather someone just say that than act like I'm an idiot.

Many pastors cling to a story about a bad experience from long ago: "This guy ran the services late and families left the church." I'm sorry that you don't have enough discernment to know who to have in your church. But don't hold all future evangelists to some stupid standard just because you had your idiot friend from Bible school come and ruin your church. That's your fault.

YOU'LL NEVER HAVE REVIVAL BECAUSE...

YOUR STAFF HATES BEING IN CHURCH

If you have a church staff that hates being in church, you'll never have revival. I've been in many meetings where people were on fire and being touched by God, but the staff couldn't stop complaining about how tired they were. Disinterested associate pastors, snide youth pastors, and angry worship teams who vocalize their fatigue will curb a revival.

I can often spot who's on staff at a church just by looking for the most disinterested people in the congregation. There's the lukewarm associate pastor in his sixties, whose greatest ambition in ministry is to collect a paycheck. He's out of shape and doesn't have enough gumption to get his suits tailored. He just sits there like a slob with his belly hanging over his belt—the least hungry person in the whole church.

Then, there's the youth pastor who sits with his arms crossed and a snide look on his face because he thinks he knows everything.

The worship team is angry and openly complains about how tired they feel. "I've been leading worship for three straight nights. My voice is gone." Maybe the problem is you're not a worship leader. You should take your acoustic guitar over to Starbucks or some indie coffee house and fulfill your dream of performing secular music in a secular venue. You're not a worshiper. Lindell Cooley in Brownsville led worship six nights a week for three years, and revival exploded. He didn't complain about being tired. If you have a staff full of losers who don't like being in church, you'll never have revival.

Sometimes, when revival hits, pastors reveal they're having issues with their staff. Pentecostal, full-gospel, charismatic churches hire pastors who don't believe in people falling under the power of God, leaving the senior pastor to address it in the middle of the biggest move of God the church has ever seen. Great job hiring a staff full of people who hate the Holy Ghost.

Years ago, I had a two-week revival in a church that shall remain nameless. The thirty-year-old children's pastor would come to the green room after service every night and complain about how tired he felt. The regular church services were usually ninety minutes, and we had been having four-and-a-half hour services, which is typical of a revival service. Finally, after the third night of relentless grumbling, my spirit had enough, and I addressed him. I asked him how long his shift would be if he worked at a daycare. He told me eight or nine hours a day. He was paid more as a children's pastor than if he was a daycare employee. So, after a few days of working a half shift as a full-time youth pastor, why are you so tired?

By the way, neither Rodney Howard-Browne nor I invented long revival services. Read the Bible. It says that Paul preached past midnight, often until one and two in the morning. I usually let out an hour or so earlier than Paul. People had more work to do back when Paul preached. They didn't have cars, so they had to walk to work the next morning.

An old preacher told me the Devil never wants a preacher to leave a service happy. At the end of a service where many people were saved and healed, this jerk would show up complaining, "I'm tired." Get him out of here!

It was discovered not long after, he was frequenting a pornography site and later dismissed from his position. It became clear why he was so tired. Maybe get some sleep instead of visiting pornographic websites after church, and revival wouldn't burn you out.

After that experience I began to pay close attention to people who are always tired. If someone responds to seeing people saved in a move of God by complaining about how tired they are, something is wrong. More people are living in sin than you may think.

It's not always associate pastors and other staff who get in the way. I've seen many senior pastors prioritize everything but revival. A pastor invited me to his church and then rescheduled because his son's soccer tournament was extended. I'll never go to that church. I'm often away from my daughter for weeks at a time while ministering in various places.

My cousin Teddy experienced a similar occurrence. The pastor called him on Saturday to tell him he might have to leave early on Sunday during his preaching, depending on the outcome of his daughter's softball game that day. He decided if they advanced in their tournament, it was more important that he and his daughter make the game than be in church on Sunday. It's not just the Devil who hinders revival, it's also lukewarm leadership.

Follow Paul's advice to Timothy. *"No one engaged in warfare entangles himself with the affairs of this life, that he may please him who enlisted him as a soldier"* (2 Timothy 2:4). Never become so distracted by commitments and events that you prioritize them over the One who called you into the ministry.

I'm not sharing these stories to vent. There is a move of God underway throughout the United States and around the world. I have two friends who are hosting massive meetings in the United States.

Pastor Rodney is having enormous meetings all through Africa and Europe. Bishop Dag Heward-Mills is holding massive crusades throughout Africa. Almost every week of the year, I travel to host revival meetings all over the country. In the same towns I visit, pastors are praying for revival. They can stop praying, they missed it. It happened just a short distance away, but they missed out because they wouldn't travel two miles to be a part of what God was doing.

Sixty-one people responded to receive Jesus Christ in one night in a town of 30,000. I'm not suggesting this is the greatest revival in world history, but what are they praying for? Sometimes you have to travel. Some people will say, "We don't have to go to another place to experience the move of God." In your case, you do because you won't allow a move of God at your own church, and you probably never will.

If you're a pastor and you've known in your spirit that it's been time to clean house for a long time, do it. Get rid of what's dead, take out the trash, and flush the toilet. You should have removed the dead weight as soon as the Lord spoke to you about it. If that's you, do it now!

I don't care if it's your worship leader. Get rid of him and play a CD in the interim. If it's your youth pastor, it would be better not to have a youth group than to keep the wrong person in leadership. Be a leader and make the tough decisions. Don't allow your staff to stifle a move of God.

YOU'LL NEVER HAVE REVIVAL BECAUSE...

YOU'RE A MONEY CONTROL FREAK

Are you a pastor who's afraid that having an evangelist visit your church will take money out of your church? Few pastors would admit it, but most view God's resources as finite. Do you liken money to a pie evangelists cut into, resulting in less funds for you? Fear of financial deficiency keeps you from having evangelists at your church.

Don't make excuses for why you don't permit evangelists to take offerings. Don't blame your disobedience to God's Word on some guy you invited in twenty years ago who did something they shouldn't have. Maybe know those who labor among you. The truth is you don't want money leaving your church.

Some pastors are professional thieves. Young evangelists take heed. Some pastors will invite you to preach when they realize that you can draw a crowd. They get dollar signs in their eyes. They plot, scheme, and use you to obtain a large offering, but in the end, they'll keep most of it for themselves.

I preached one night at an Italian Pentecostal church in Montreal, Quebec, and received a check for $1,000. After service, I remember asking Adalis, "What do I have to do to have a financial breakthrough? I fasted and prayed. We saw people saved. We had major miracles. It was one of the best services I've ever had." I lost money taking the trip from Virginia to Montreal, so I thought for sure something was going to break financially.

Years later, when the new pastor took over that church, the bookkeeper reported that the previous pastor told him to keep $10,000 for the church and give me $1,000. You go to Hell for that kind of thing. That pastor is no longer with us on planet Earth—he died early. He was a thief who touched the Lord's money. Whatever mistakes I've made in life, I promise you I've never done something like that, and I never will. I'd mug an old woman on the street before I'd touch a dollar of God's money.

Do you want your people blessed? Many ministers consider themselves conservative but handle money like a socialist. They reason in their minds, 'Why does that young guy need all that money?' It's none of your business.

Do you set honorariums for speakers? Do you give your staff raises when they have children or get married instead of basing it on performance and cost of living? That's

Marxist ideology. Holding on so tightly to money will not foster a financial breakthrough. You'll never have abundance if this is your attitude.

Where is the concept of an honorarium in the Bible? The Bible says to let each man give as he's directed by the Spirit (2 Corinthians 9:7). What part of that do you not understand? Nowhere in the Bible does it say to let the board of directors determine what a pastor should receive. The offering is an opportunity for church people to be blessed. Likewise, your opportunity to receive a financial blessing comes in your giving to the work of other ministries. There should be money that leaves your church in bulk to fund the work of other ministries. If you do that, you'll change levels. If you don't, you'll stay the same.

Any evangelist of worth has experienced this scenario: A meeting is growing, God is moving, there are plenty of people in the congregation, and people are being saved. But rather than extend something that is obviously working, the church ends the meetings on the scheduled date because they are nervous about reducing their future Sunday offerings. This kind of thinking hinders revival.

Let me retell a story that demonstrates what can happen when you stop worrying about the offering. Lester Sumrall shared about a time when Oral Roberts visited South Bend, Indiana, to hold a partners meeting. He had over 3000 partners in attendance, most of whom were from Lester Sumrall's church. When Oral Roberts gave a call for people who would pledge a minimum of $1000, Pastor Sumrall's entire congregation came forward. Then, Oral Roberts asked that they come to the altar holding up one finger for every thousand dollars they were prepared to give. Again, Lester Sumrall's entire congregation came forward with all ten fingers raised. Keep in mind, this was in the 1970s when $10,000 was worth upwards of $75,000 today.

After the partners' meeting, Lester Sumrall was convinced he would have to resign because Oral Roberts had effectively taken all the money out of South Bend. He wasn't angry or bitter about it. He had no issue with the money going to Oral Roberts' ministry, but practically speaking, he didn't see how he could continue to do what God called him to do.

He wrote his resignation letter and then had an idea. He planned to take a final offering as a fleece before the Lord, and then he would turn in his letter. He instructed his ushers to take the offering and present him with the final count. The ushers presented him with the final numbers with tears in their eyes. They had just received the largest offering in the history of the church.

When an evangelist teaches on giving, the giving doesn't stop when he leaves town. A true evangelist will help your church grow spiritually, physically, and financially. God uses evangelists to create breakthroughs in the area of giving.

Twelve years ago, I held a three-week revival meeting in which a man's son was healed of Tourette's syndrome. Recently, that same man called to tell me how much he had hated offerings before hearing me preach. He hated giving and didn't tithe, but after his son was healed, he gave the largest check he'd ever given. All these years later, he still attends that same church. I received the initial offering, but the pastor of that church has received that man's tithes for the past twelve years. The pastor also had six employees at the time I preached there, and now he has thirty-four people on staff.

If you're a pastor, get out of the habit of thinking short-term. Intelligent people don't make short-term decisions, they make decisions that have a lasting impact.

When I invited Jesse Duplantis to our church, a wealthy man gave ninety percent of his income in the offering. His job was being threatened by a person in leadership who didn't like him, and he sowed in faith for a resolution. He didn't give it to me; he gave it to Jesse Duplantis' ministry. If I were the average pastor, I would have thought, 'He comes to my church, and he's never given me an offering of that magnitude.' But people are free to give as they are directed by the Spirit.

The following week, the wealthy member of my church received a call informing him the person trying to have him fired had been dismissed. They offered him a position on the leadership team, which came with a substantial raise. Jesse received one offering, but that man is a tither who comes to my church and gives continually.

Quit striving for your piece of the pie. Stop dropping hints around rich people about what other well-off people have given to pressure them into giving to your building program. That's a worldly perspective. You'll never have any money if you use tactics like that. You're trying to gather up quail rather than allowing the Lord to rain quail down from Heaven.

People should give as directed by the Holy Spirit in the direction that the Holy Spirit leads. God will bring an evangelist to your church to provide your congregation an opportunity to sow into something outside the church that will cause the blessing of God to overtake them. Honorariums destroy that. When you limit the offering, you limit your people's opportunities for blessing.

Just for the record, I've given $100,000 upfront to multiple evangelists I've invited to my church. I don't think anyone has received less than $30,000 to preach at Revival Today Church. Some only came for one night. In addition, I instructed them to receive an offering for their ministry. I even request they use their own offering envelopes. One of my greatest joys as a pastor is treating evangelists honorably and not being afraid of them.

I don't care if Jesse Duplantis uses his own envelopes and gets the contact information of people from my church. They're not his people, and they're not mine—they're

God's people. I shepherd those He entrusts me to shepherd. If you know of an evangelist who took everybody's names off a list and used that information to start a church next door or ask them about partnership, don't have an evangelist who would do something like that. I have a strong feeling Jesse Duplantis isn't going to move to Pittsburgh and start a "spite church" a mile away from me. But if he does, I'd be very happy because I'd be able to hang out with him more than I do now.

The bottom line is this: if you don't believe in sowing and reaping, you can't have revival. You're stingy, and God detests stingy people. David was not stingy, and neither was Abraham. Abraham was at the door of his tent, looking for people to feed. The Bible says, *"There is one who scatters, yet increases more; and there is one who withholds more than is right, but it leads to poverty"* (Proverbs 11:24). A statement written by Solomon, the richest man who ever lived.

You won't get anywhere by prioritizing your building program over inviting an evangelist to hold a revival. Enjoy your twenty-year building program and your mortgage. Meanwhile, I gave lavishly while building our church. The more I gave, the more land we acquired. I've proved this theory many times over because it's based on the Word of God, and it works.

Stop thinking about the amount of money that leaves your church. I purposed in my heart to give a million dollars to

Pastor Rodney's ministry. I told the Lord that as soon as our account reached $3 million, I would sow $1 million. Within weeks we hit the target, and I sowed the million immediately. We've been operating in a billion-dollar flow ever since. If you're wondering what a billion-dollar flow is, allow me to break it down. Although we don't presently have $1 billion in the bank, there's nothing someone with a billion dollars in the bank could do that we can't do.

But do it your way. Keep trying to hold on to all the money and let me know how it works out for you. When we started making $100,000 the standard seed of our ministry, buildings, and land began pouring into our possession like sweaters from Walmart. But maybe you know best.

YOU'LL NEVER HAVE REVIVAL BECAUSE...

YOU HATE THE HOLY GHOST

No one would outwardly admit this, but some pastors harbor hatred towards the Holy Ghost. Do you dislike speaking in tongues and people falling under the power? Do you get nervous when the sick receive prayer? Do all manifestations of the Spirit bother you? It's because you hate the Holy Spirit. You haven't anointed anyone with oil in so long that the oil has gone rancid in the jar. You prefer a nice, clean service—a religious eighty-five-minute Ted Talk.

In many churches, the catchers look like they're in their mid-hundreds. The last time anyone prayed for the sick or laid hands on people was during World War II. You can always tell the last time a church had a move of God by the age of the catchers.

When revival broke out at Asbury University in Kentucky, we had a bird's eye view of this attitude towards the Holy

Spirit. People weren't even falling out under the power or speaking in tongues, but many were bothered by and judgmental towards students worshiping for an extended time.

There are Christians who mock believers who fall out under the power. Many churches that used to be Word of Faith, Charismatic, or Pentecostal are nothing more than mainstream churches. They believe in healing and manifestations of the Holy Spirit on paper only. There's been zero evidence of the Holy Spirit at their church in over twenty years.

The Bible says, *"Having a form of godliness but rejecting the power. Have nothing to do with people like that"* (2 Timothy 3:5 KJV).

YOU'LL NEVER HAVE REVIVAL BECAUSE...

YOU CHOOSE GUEST SPEAKERS INSTEAD OF EVANGELISTS

This one is for both pastors and evangelists. There's a difference between an evangelist and a guest speaker. An evangelist isn't a traveling speaker. An evangelist is gifted, like Philip, to not only win the lost but preach and electrify entire cities with the power of God.

> And the people with one accord gave heed unto those things which Philip spake, hearing and seeing the miracles which he did. For unclean spirits, crying with loud voice, came out of many that were possessed with them:

> and many taken with palsies, and that were lame, were healed. And there was great joy in that city.
>
> — ACTS 8:6-8 (KJV)

An evangelist preaches Christ unto men, but he also works the work of Christ and brings joy to a city. Why have you never had revival in your city? Bring in an evangelist who has revivals and allow him to be led by the Holy Ghost. I don't try to *have* a revival; I *carry* revival.

Our ministry is named Revival Today because it's who we are; we're a ministry in revival. I'm not a one-or-two-night conference speaker. I hold meetings Sunday through Friday, and whenever possible, I preach 10:30 AM and 7:00 PM services. If you study church history, you'll find evangelists always taught during the day and preached at night. That's revival!

Revival is not a conference with a six-speaker lineup over the course of a week. That's the equivalent of six guys in a canoe, all paddling in different directions. That's not revival. None of them stay for the other speaker's services, so they have no idea what the last person said. There's no continuity or flow. They are like guests on a talk show.

You are never going to have a revival with six guest speakers. Some of them may preach oppositional doctrines. One guy might preach on prosperity, while another attacks it. If you're a pastor, you need to keep this in mind before you schedule your next event.

I have a question for evangelists: What is your ministry's primary focus? Is it ushering revival or booking guest speaking engagements? You need to be clear about your calling and avoid taking meetings where you're expected to perform as a "guest speaker." Your job is to preach Christ unto men.

Father, I pray everyone reading this book will find and remain in the center of Your will for their lives. I pray no one will miss your final move on the Earth, in Jesus' name, Amen.

AFTERWORD

My sister-in-Christ, Vicki Hankins, is the founding pastor of Church in the City, a sizable church in the Dallas area. When I held meetings there, she never gave me any instructions regarding how long the service should be or about taking offerings. When the meetings ended, I looked at the financial report and noticed that no one put more in the offerings than she did personally—not even the church itself. The church gave as well, but she gave of her own money.

She's a wealthy woman who came from nothing. People like her are always strong givers, and they're not stingy. She looks ten years younger than her age because of God's blessing.

When she saw how full the church was, she suggested we extend the meeting another week. People like her don't worry about anything—they're easygoing.

Then you have pastors with thirty people in their church who worry about what the attendance will be if they extend it for a week. No one's showing up as it is, so what are you really afraid of? Your church is only thirty people away from being empty. Why not take a risk? Why not make an aggressive move of faith and see what happens rather than trying to cling to what little you have?

What's the point of worrying an evangelist will take all your money when you're already broke? Why are you worried about losing money? Why are you worried about an evangelist taking your money when you've already found a way to lose it all without him?

Fear.

A pastor who won't bring in evangelists because he fears too much money will leave his church is like a poor woman living in section eight housing with her boyfriend. After learning about Jesus, she's excited and believes, but is unwilling to take the risk and act according to her faith. Even though she's miserable in her current condition, she's comfortable. She knows how to live in a trailer. She doesn't know what will happen if she leaves her boyfriend, finds a job, and no longer qualifies for government assistance and section-eight housing. The thought is unfamiliar to her. She prefers to remain in her squalor rather than take a step of faith in God's Word and discover where it leads.

If you're a pastor reading this, I challenge you to take a step of faith in God's Word. You can be the seventy-five-year-

AFTERWORD

old pastor who wonders what could have happened if you gave it your all, or you can sit back at seventy-five years old and know you gave God your best. Take the risk and watch what happens. God likes people who take risks. When you do, God will help you.

I wrote this book because I don't want you to miss revival. I want you to be a part of this final move of God that's clearly underway. I'm not going to miss it. How about you?

"My generation shall be saved!"

— JONATHAN SHUTTLESWORTH

ABOUT THE AUTHOR

Evangelist and Pastor, Jonathan Shuttlesworth, is the founder of Revival Today and Pastor of Revival Today Church, ministries dedicated to reaching lost and hurting people with The Gospel of Jesus Christ.

In fulfilling his calling, Jonathan Shuttlesworth has conducted meetings and open-air crusades throughout North America, India, the Caribbean, and Central and South Africa.

Revival Today Church was launched in 2022 as a soul-winning, Holy Spirit-honoring church that is unapologetic about believing the Bible to bless families and nations.

Each day thousands of lives are impacted globally through Revival Today Broadcasting and Revival Today Church, located in Pittsburgh, Pennsylvania.

While methods may change, Revival Today's heartbeat remains for the lost, providing biblical teaching on faith, healing, prosperity, freedom from sin, and living a victorious life.

If you need help or would like to partner with Revival Today to see this generation and nation transformed through The Gospel, follow these links…

www.RevivalToday.com
www.RevivalTodayChurch.com

Get access to our 24/7 network Revival Today Global Broadcast. Download the Revival Today app in your Apple App Store or Google Play Store. Watch live on Apple TV, Roku, Amazon Fire TV, and Android TV.

Call: 412-787-2578

- facebook.com/revivaltoday
- x.com/jdshuttlesworth
- instagram.com/jdshuttlesworth
- youtube.com/@jonathanshuttlesworth

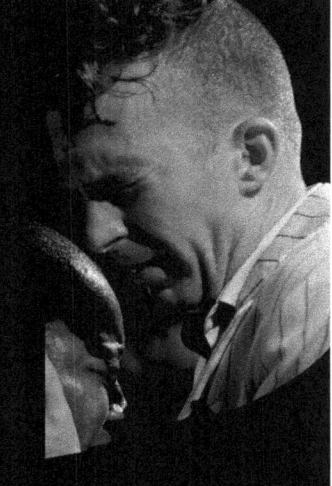

DO SOMETHING TODAY THAT WILL CHANGE YOUR LIFE FOREVER

THUS SAITH THE LORD, **MAKE THIS VALLEY FULL OF DITCHES**. FOR THUS SAITH THE LORD, YE SHALL NOT SEE WIND, NEITHER SHALL YE SEE RAIN; YET THAT VALLEY SHALL BE FILLED WITH WATER... **THIS IS BUT A LIGHT THING IN THE SIGHT OF THE LORD**... AND IT CAME TO PASS... **THE COUNTRY WAS FILLED WITH WATER.**

2 KINGS 3:16-18; 20

Revival is the only answer to the problems of this country - nothing more, nothing less, nothing else.

Thank you for standing with me as a partner with Revival Today. We must see this nation shaken by the power of God.

You cannot ask God to bless you first, prior to giving. God asks you to step out first in your giving - and then He makes it rain. We are believing God for 1,000 people to partner with us monthly at $84. Something everyone can do, but a significant seed that will connect you to the rainmaker.

IF YOU HAVE NOT YET PARTNERED WITH REVIVAL TODAY, JOIN US TODAY!

This year is not your year to dig small ditches. When I grew tired of small meetings and altar calls, I moved forward in faith and God responded. God is the rainmaker, but you must give Him something to fill. It's time for you to move forward! **Will you stand with me today to see the nations of the world shaken by the power of God?**

Revivaltoday.com/give

PayPal
revivaltoday.com/paypal

Zelle® info@revivaltoday.com

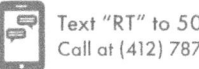 @RTgive

Text "RT" to 50155
Call at (412) 787-2578

Mail a check to:

Revival Today P.O. BOX 7
PROSPERITY PA 15329

REVIVAL TODAY   Email: info@revivaltoday.com

www.ingramcontent.com/pod-product-compliance
Lightning Source LLC
LaVergne TN
LVHW010304070426
835507LV00033B/3500